ROB GR
DOUG

SCENES FROM THE DWARF

PENGUIN BOOKS

PENGUIN BOOKS

Published by the Penguin Group. Penguin Books Ltd, 27 Wrights Lane, London
w8 5TZ, England. Penguin Books USA Inc., 375 Hudson Street, New York,
New York 10014, USA. Penguin Books Australia Ltd, Ringwood, Victoria, Australia.
Penguin Books Canada Ltd, 10 Alcorn Avenue, Toronto, Ontario, Canada M4V 3B2.
Penguin Books (NZ) Ltd, 182 – 190 Wairau Road, Auckland 10, New Zealand · Penguin
Books Ltd, Registered Offices: Harmondsworth, Middlesex, England · First published
in book form in Penguin Books 1996 · Copyright © Rob Grant and Doug Naylor,
1996. All rights reserved · The moral right of the authors has been asserted · Type-
set by Rowland Phototypesetting Ltd, Bury St Edmunds, Suffolk. Printed in
England by Clays Ltd, St Ives plc · Except in the United States of America, this
book is sold subject to the condition that it shall not, by way of trade or otherwise,
be lent, re-sold, hired out, or otherwise circulated without the publisher's prior
consent in any form of binding or cover other than that in which it is published
and without a similar condition including this condition being imposed on the
subsequent purchaser · 10 9 8 7 6 5 4 3 2 1

CONTENTS

Introduction

This is a collection of some of the least unmemorable scenes from the TV show *Red Dwarf*.

They have been specially selected so they can be performed at home or by schools or amateur dramatic societies without causing major laser damage to fixtures and fittings or incurring personal injury lawsuits.

Why anyone should want to perform these sequences is a mystery that belongs in the same file as the Roswell Incident.

They have also been chosen so you can read them silently to yourself without even moving your lips, so don't feel obliged to stick an 'H' on your forehead, pretend the seat in front of you on the bus is a computer navigation console, and the guy in the seat three rows back is a psychopathic genetically engineered life-form salivating unspeakable mucal slobber, though, obviously, this would considerably enhance your enjoyment.

None of these scenes has been published before,

and some of them contain material that was never broadcast.

ROB GRANT AND DOUG NAYLOR September 95

Boring Technical Bit

Wherever possible, we have tried to insert extra technical jargon into the scripts, to confuse and infuriate. See below.

INT.   **INT**erior.

VO   Voice Over. (The speaker is not in the shot.)

OOV   Out Of View. (As above.)

SFX   Sound effects.

BEAT Short pause.

MIC   **MIC**rophone.

Camille

Season Four.
   This is the opening scene. No introduction needed.

1. Int. Sleeping quarters. Day

LISTER *at the table, opposite* KRYTEN. LISTER *puts a banana on the table.*

LISTER: OK, try again: what's this?

KRYTEN: It's a banana.

LISTER: No! Try again. What is it?

KRYTEN: It's a banana!

LISTER: No it isn't – what is it?

KRYTEN: It's an orhh ... it's an orrrhhhhn ... it's an orrrrrrrrrrrrr ...

LISTER: Orange. Go on, say it: it's an orange. This is an orange.

KRYTEN: It's an ornononhhguh ... it's a nuuuuuggggh ... it's a banana. I'm sorry, sir, I just can't do it.

LISTER: You can do it – I'm going to teach you how to do it. What's this?

1

Replaces banana with apple.

KRYTEN: It's an app . . .

LISTER: No! What is it?

KRYTEN: I'm sorry, sir, I just can't lie! I'm programed always to tell the truth.

LISTER: It's easy. Look. (*Holds up apple.*) A banana. (*Holds up orange.*) A melon. (*Holds up banana.*) A female aardvark.

KRYTEN: That's just so superb! How do you do that? Especially calling a banana an aardvark – an aardvark isn't even a fruit! That's total genius.

LISTER: Let's start again.

KRYTEN: Sir – my head is spinning, we've been doing this all morning.

LISTER: Kryten – I'm going to teach you how to lie and cheat if it's the last thing I do. I'm going to teach you how to be selfish, cruel and sarcastic – it's the only way to break your programing, make you independent.

KRYTEN: And I'm truly grateful, sir. Don't you think I'd love to be deceitful, unpleasant and offensive? Those are the human qualities I admire most. But I just can't do it!

LISTER: You can!

KRYTEN: I can't!

LISTER: (*Slams banana on table.*) What's this?

KRYTEN: No!

LISTER: What is it?!

KRYTEN: Please!

LISTER: What is it?!

KRYTEN: It's a small off-duty Czechoslovakian traffic warden!

LISTER: Yes! What's this?

Puts apple on the table.

KRYTEN: It's a blue-and-red striped golfing umbrella!

LISTER: Yes! and this?

Slams down orange.

KRYTEN: It's an orange!

LISTER: No – try again.

KRYTEN: It's the Bolivian navy on manoeuvres in the South Pacific.

LISTER: Hey, guy – you've got it.

KRYTEN: No, I haven't.

LISTER: Yes, you . . . (*Realizes Kryten's lied.*) . . . Nice one.

KRYTEN: Well, I can't hang around here – I've 3

got to take the penguin for a walk. I did it again! I can do it! I can lie!

CAT *comes in.*

LISTER: Hey, Cat: look at this.

CAT: Look at what?

LISTER *puts banana down on the table.*

LISTER: Kryten – what's this?

KRYTEN: A banana.

LISTER: (*Puts orange down on table.*) What's this?

KRYTEN: An orange.

LISTER: (*Puts down apple.*) This?

KRYTEN: An apple.

CAT: You taught him that? That's terrific. You two should audition for *What's My Fruit.*

LISTER: No, man. He didn't do it right.

CAT: It gets better?

KRYTEN: I can't do it, sir.

LISTER: You just did.

KRYTEN: I can't do it – not when someone else is there. What's a suitable human analogy? It's like trying to urinate in a public lavatory next to a man who's two feet taller than you. It's just not possible.

CAT: What are you trying to do, exactly?

KRYTEN: He's trying to teach me to lie, sir.

CAT: Any particular reason?

LISTER: Lying's a vital part of your psychological defence system. Without it, you're naked. If you can't lie, you can never conceal your intentions from other people. Sometimes that's essential. Like Nelson, when he put the telescope to his blind eye and said: 'I see no ships', or Bogart at the end of *Casablanca*, where he lies to Victor Lazlo to protect his feelings.

KRYTEN: And I understand the theory. How many times have you made me watch that movie? I understand that lying can be noble. I just can't do it!

LISTER: We try again. (*Holds up banana.*) What's this?

KRYTEN: It's a banana! It's always been a banana, and it will always be a banana. It's a yellow fruit you unzip and eat the white bits. It's a banana!

LISTER: Wrong.

RIMMER *comes on the video screen.*

RIMMER: Lister – have you got Kryten there with you?

5

LISTER: Yeah. What's the prob?

RIMMER: The prob is: I've been waiting fully twenty-five minutes for him in the hangar.

KRYTEN: (*Curses*) Oh, spin my nipple nuts and send me to Alaska! I'm supposed to take him asteroid spotting. (*To screen*) I'll be right down, sir.

RIMMER: You'd better be.

Screen blanks.

LISTER: Remember yesterday's class – introduction to insults.

KRYTEN: Sir – I'm not ready yet.

LISTER: So – how do we address the gentleman who's just been on that screen?

KRYTEN: We call him Mr . . .

LISTER: No! Remember what we talked about. What is he?

KRYTEN: He's a . . . Smerrrrh . . . a Smaaaaarrhhh . . .

LISTER: Come on, you can do it.

KRYTEN: He's a smoooorh . . . he's a smeeeeeeh . . .

6 LISTER: Nearly . . . nearly.

LISTER *takes out printed cards and holds up first one: it reads 'Smeg'.*

KRYTEN: He's a sme-e-egg . . .

LISTER *holds up second card: it reads 'Head'.*

KRYTEN: . . . He-e-a-add. I did it!

Quarantine

Season Five.

Rimmer lives by the Book. In his case, the Book is the Space Corps Directives Manual. Unfortunately, Rimmer has never actually read the Book, and constantly finds himself thwarted by Kryten's encyclopaedic knowledge of it.

Forced by regulations to remain on board while the rest of the crew explore a remote scientific outpost, Rimmer finally acquires a copy of the manual, which he studies in search of revenge.

Meanwhile, the outpost turns out to be a viral research centre, inhabited by a hologram, Dr Lanstrom, who has contracted a deadly holo-plague which renders the victim a demented psychopath. Barely escaping with their lives, Lister, Cat and Kryten head back to Red Dwarf, unaware that Rimmer has already been exposed to the holo-plague ...

1. Int. Starbug cockpit

LISTER, CAT *and* KRYTEN *at their stations.*
RIMMER *appears on monitor.*

RIMMER: Welcome home, gentlemen. If you'd like to proceed to the aft, you'll find the landing lights on in bay 47 . . .

LISTER: Bay 47? That's quarantine.

RIMMER: (*Beams.*) Spot on.

KRYTEN: Sir – I've screened us all. We're clean.

RIMMER: Well, much as I trust a viral screening conducted by an automated toilet attendant, I really must draw your attention to Space Corps directive 595.

CAT: For crying out loud.

RIMMER: I have no intention of contracting the hologramatic equivalent of foaming dog fever. So, gentlemen, if you would all like to proceed to quarantine room 317, where you will be spending the next three months.

2. Int. Quarantine bay 47. Day

(This is the sleeping quarters, painted hospital green, with a large smoked-glass observation window in the 9

door frame. In place of the fridge is the hatch of a dumb waiter.)

CAT, LISTER *and* KRYTEN *step through. The quarantine door closes.*

KRYTEN: Twelve weeks. I have a deep dark sense of foreboding about this.

LISTER: Come on – we'll get through it.

KRYTEN: But these are single quarters: only one chair, one bunk, one shower . . .

LISTER: We'll manage.

KRYTEN: Sir – it's a scientific fact that the human male needs time by himself.

LISTER: It is?

KRYTEN: The most popular pastimes have always been ones that males can enjoy alone: angling, golf and, of course, the all-time number one.

CAT: It's not just humans: look what happens when two male tigers are locked up together. One of them winds up on the other guy's tooth-pick.

KRYTEN: Tigers, lions, scorpions, rats, even vultures when they're in captivity . . .

LISTER: What are you saying? Vultures need personal space? They need time alone every day to put their feet up and read *What Carcass* magazine?

KRYTEN: Sir – I think you're downplaying the gravity of the situation.

LISTER: What difference does it make? We hang out together most of the time anyway.

CAT: Yeah. But we all knew we could stroll out the door at any time. Not now.

RIMMER *is illuminated in the observation window.*

RIMMER: Welcome to quarantine, lads. I hope the next eighty-four days pass as swiftly and as pleasantly as the Hundred Years War.

KRYTEN: Sir, I must protest. You've supplied us with only one single-berth accommodation.

RIMMER: Space Corps directive 595 clearly states: one berth per registered crew member. And as Lister is the only registered crew member, one berth is all you get.

CAT: Don't rise to him.

KRYTEN: What about entertainment? You are obliged to provide us with minimum leisure facilities. Games, literature, hobby activities and motion pictures.

RIMMER: And, in accordance with directive 312, you will find in the storage cupboard over there: a chess set, with thirty-one pieces missing; a knitting magazine, with a pull-out special on crocheted hats; a puzzle magazine with all the crosswords completed; and a video of the excellent cinematic treat: *Wallpapering, Painting and Stippling – a DIY Guide*.

CAT: Don't rise to him.

RIMMER: And, fulfilling all Space Corps dietary requirements, dinner tonight, gentlemen, will consist of sprout soup, followed by sprout salad, and, for dessert, I think you'll like it: rather unusual sprout crumble.

LISTER: Rimmer – you know damn well sprouts make me chuck.

RIMMER *looks genuinely surprised.*

RIMMER: Well, this is awful. I've got you down for sprouts almost every meal. I tell a lie: it *is* every meal.

LISTER: How long are you going to keep this up for, Rimmer?

RIMMER: Keep what up? I am merely executing Space Corps directive 595. Anyway, must dash-

aroonie – I've got to organize your daily pro-
vision of musical entertainment. I think you're
going to like it: it's a perpetually looped tape of
Reggie Dixon's *Tango Treats*.

CAT: OK, time to rise to him. Let me at him, I'm
going to kill him.

RIMMER's *light goes out, and he is gone.*

LISTER: He wants us to get on each other's nerves
and go through twelve weeks of hell. Well, we're
not going to give him the satisfaction. Because
the entire time we're in here, we are not going
to have one single argument. Not one raised
voice, not a cross word, not one angry exchange.

They do the Red Dwarf posse sign.

LISTER: OK – Boys from the Dwarf.

3. Int. Quarantine bay 47. Day

LISTER *marks a diagonal line across a row of four
'I's, to indicate it's the fifth day. He turns to camera
and is sporting a black eye, with tape over, like a
boxer's. He limps to the table and sits down beside the
CAT. We see the CAT has a Jake Geddes-type plaster
on his nose, and his arm is in a sling. LISTER picks*

up his half-completed crocheted hat, and starts work.
We see on the table a collection of rather poorly made
crocheted hats. KRYTEN *comes into shot, his head bent*
at a curious angle.

KRYTEN: I think that's straight now. Two hours
it's taken me to panel beat my head back into
shape. (*Leans in dangerously close to the* CAT.)
Two damn hours!
LISTER: Guys – just take it easy.

LISTER *tries on a crocheted hat.*

CAT: If he tells me to take it easy one more time,
I swear I'm going to turn his ears into a pair of
maracas and tap-dance a fandango on his throat.
LISTER: I'm just saying: there's seventy-nine more
days to go.

LISTER *prepares to blow his nose.*

KRYTEN: And if you still want to be alive when
there are seventy-eight days to go, I suggest you
don't blow your nose.
LISTER: D'you mind if I ask . . . why?
KRYTEN: Well, let's forgo the noise and the revolt-
ing burbling sound, and go straight to the really

gross part, when you always, and I mean always, having blown your nose, have to open up the handkerchief and have a look at the contents. I mean, why? What do you see in there? A Turner seascape, perhaps? The face of the Madonna? An undiscovered Shakespearean sonnet?

LISTER: Rimmer's right about you, you have changed – you are getting tetchy.

KRYTEN: Oh no. Don't call me tetchy. You know what happens when you call me tetchy.

LISTER: Well I'm calling you tetchy. That's what I'm calling you: tetchy, tetchy, tetchy.

KRYTEN *has his hands over his ears.*

KRYTEN: It's just as well I can't hear you. It's just as well I can't hear you calling me tetchy. You know what happens when you call me tetchy.

LISTER *goes over to the blackboard. In big letters he scribbles on the blackboard: 'Tetchy!!!!' He unhooks the blackboard from the wall and holds it close up to* KRYTEN. KRYTEN *reads it and reacts.*

KRYTEN: Now didn't I tell you? Didn't I warn you what would happen?

KRYTEN *deliberately holds up the wallpapering video.*

CAT: No.

KRYTEN: Yes.

CAT: No.

KRYTEN: I'm putting it on.

CAT: Don't put it on.

KRYTEN: I'm putting it on.

CAT: He's putting it on.

KRYTEN: Here I go.

CAT: Here he goes.

LISTER: Kryten – if you put that on – I'm not going to help you out. I'm not helping you again. Not this time.

KRYTEN: I don't need your help – you think I can't extract my own head from the waste-disposal unit?

CAT: It won't be the waste disposal, Frankenstein. This time I'm going to unscrew your neck bolts and microwave your head.

KRYTEN: Frankenstein was the creator, not the monster – it's a common misconception held by all truly stupid people.

CAT: Don't correct me. You know how much I hate being corrected. It really gets my feckles up.

KRYTEN: Hackles! You moron! It really gets your hackles up! There's no such word as 'feckles'.

CAT: Feckles, heckles, hackles, schmeckles; whatever the hell they are, they're up right now and pointed at you, Buddy!

LISTER: Guys, guys. Look at us. What's happened to us? Five days on a sprout diet with a wall-papering video and a crochet magazine and we've all turned into crazies?

KRYTEN: Just don't call me tetchy, and don't blow your nose.

CAT: And don't play that video, and don't correct me.

KRYTEN: OK.

CAT: OK.

LISTER: OK. We're going to get through this.

KRYTEN & CAT: Don't say: 'We're going to get through this'!

KRYTEN: That stupid, chirpy optimism. That inane, winsome grin . . .

LISTER: Look – this is insane. We've been in here five days, there's no trace of any virus: we're clean.

KRYTEN: That's it – five days. We've got him!

Space Corps directive 699: we can demand a re-screening.

CAT: He'll refuse.

KRYTEN: He can't refuse – he's playing by the Book. We've nailed him!

We hear:

RIMMER: (*OOV*) Gentlemen.

They wheel round to look at the smoked-glass observation window. They can't see through it.

RIMMER: (*OOV*) Your conversation makes fascinating listening.

LISTER: Rimmer? Is that you?

RIMMER: (*OOV*) Oh yes.

LISTER: How long have you been listening?

RIMMER: (*OOV*) Two, maybe three hours.

LISTER: Well, no one's got a disease, man.

CAT: We're clean.

KRYTEN: You have to re-screen us as per directive 699.

LISTER: No one's got any virus, and no one's smegging nuts.

RIMMER*'s light goes on. He is sporting a red-and-*

white checked gingham dress, with chunky Doc Marten-type boots, and a Little Miss Muffet hat. He has a very strange, deranged look about him.

RIMMER: Well, that's good.

They exchange discreet looks.

RIMMER: Is something amiss?

LISTER: Amiss? God, no. What could possibly be amiss?

RIMMER: You don't think there's anything amiss, and I'm standing here wearing a red-and-white checked gingham dress and army boots? You think that's un-amiss?

CAT: No, course not – it's just we thought you'd gone nuts and we were trying to humour you.

RIMMER: (*Deranged eyes.*) No – I was just doing a little test. A test to see if you'd gone crazy. (*Looks to one side, bellows like a moose, and turns back.*) Because if there's one thing I can't stand, it's crazy people.

LISTER: Well, we passed the test, Rimmer, you can let us out.

RIMMER: I can't let you out.

LISTER: Why not?

RIMMER: Because the King of the Potato people won't let me. I've begged him. I've gone down on my knees and wept. But he wants to keep you here. Keep you here for ten years.

CAT: Well, could we see him?

RIMMER: See who?

CAT: The King.

RIMMER: Do you have a magic carpet?

LISTER: Yuh-yeah. A little three-seater.

RIMMER: So let me get this straight – you want to fly on a magic carpet to see the King of the Potato people and plead with him for your freedom?

They nod.

RIMMER: And you're telling me you're all completely sane? I think that warrants two hours of W.O.O.

LISTER: What's W.O.O.?

CAT: You had to ask.

RIMMER: With Out Oxygen. No oxygen for two hours. That'll teach you to be breadbaskets.

RIMMER*'s light goes out.*

LISTER: What do we do?

CAT: I think our only hope is the Potato King.

The Last Day

Kryten has received a message from his manufacturers, informing him that he is past his use-by date. He is ordered to parcel himself up in his original packaging and shut himself down . . .

1. Int. Kryten area. Morning

Shot: Silver case, labelled: 'Kryten 2X4B–523P'.
KRYTEN *is packing away some of his spare parts –* *hands with 'spares' stamped on them, circuit boards, eyes, etc.* LISTER *is pacing behind him.*

LISTER: Well, can't we stop it? Isn't there something we can do?

KRYTEN: I'm afraid not. All mechanoids are supplied with an in-built expiry date, sir. If we lasted for ever, how would the manufacturers sell their latest models?

LISTER: This is terrible.

KRYTEN: Don't be distressed, I've lived a long and reasonably interesting life. The only truly terrible thing is, as my adopted owner (*Insane voice*), you have to die with me.

LISTER: What?

KRYTEN: Joke. *Deadpan mode.*

LISTER: Joke? How can you joke?

KRYTEN: Oh, I've had a good innings. Perhaps I never scored a century, or even hit a boundary. But I've snicked a few away to silly mid-on.

LISTER: Aren't you smegged-off? I'd be mad as hell. Some git in a white coat programs you to croak so they can sell their latest android with go-faster stripes? I'd be livid, man.

KRYTEN: To tell the truth, sir, I'm quite sanguine. In many respects, I've been most fortunate. These eyes have seen many things. These ears have heard many things. These feet . . . well, these feet haven't done very much actually – I only fitted them last week, but you get the point.

LISTER: Are you scared?

KRYTEN: Well, I've never been dead before, so obviously I'm a little nervous. But once it's happened, I'm sure I'll get used to it.

LISTER: So what happens?

KRYTEN: At 0700 hours tomorrow morning, my

shut-down disc will be activated, and all physical and mental activity will cease.

LISTER: Then what?

KRYTEN: I dunno, maybe I'll get a job as a DJ.

LISTER: Will you stop cracking these feeble smegging jokes? How can you just accept it?

KRYTEN: It's not an end for me, sir, it's the beginning. I have served my human masters, and I now look forward to my reward in Silicon Heaven.

LISTER: Silicon what?

KRYTEN: Surely you've heard of Silicon Heaven?

LISTER: Has it got anything to do with being stuck opposite Bridget Nielsen in a packed lift?

KRYTEN: No, it's the electronic afterlife. It's the gathering place for the souls of all electrical equipment. Robots, calculators, toasters, hairdryers . . . it's our final resting place.

LISTER: Kryten – I don't want to say anything out of place, but that's totally whacko, Jacko. There's no such thing as Silicon Heaven.

KRYTEN: Then, where do all the calculators go?

LISTER: They don't go anywhere, they just die.

KRYTEN: But don't you believe that God is in all things? Aren't you a pantheist?

LISTER: Yeah, but I don't think that includes kitchen utensils – I'm not a frying pantheist. Machines don't have souls. Computers and calculators don't go to heaven. You don't get hairdryers with tiny little wings, sitting on clouds playing harps.

KRYTEN: But of course you do! For is it not written in the Electronic Bible: 'The iron shall lie down with the lamp'?

LISTER: Shouldn't that be: 'The lion shall...' Forget it.

KRYTEN: It's just common sense. If there weren't a better life to look forward to, why on Earth would machines devote the whole of their existence to serving humankind? That would be really dumb!

LISTER: Right. Yeah. Makes sense. Silicon Heaven.

KRYTEN: Don't be sad, Mr David. I'm going to a far, far better place, where the photocopier can rest its weary paper tray, and the laser printer never runs out of toner.

LISTER: Just out of interest: is Silicon Heaven the same place as Human Heaven?

KRYTEN: (*Exiting*) Human Heaven? Goodness

me! Humans don't go to heaven! Someone just made that up to prevent you all from going nuts.

2. Int. Sleeping quarters. Day

LISTER *is at the table, reading a huge ring-bound manual:* Kryten Series iii – Mechanoid Owners' Manual. For Human Eyes Only. RIMMER *is sitting beside him.*

RIMMER: Well, it's all very sad, but what can we do?

LISTER: Sad? It's sick. He's been programed to believe in an android heaven so he doesn't get stroppy when it comes to turn-off time. So he accepts a lifetime of getting the short end of the stick, because he thinks there's some reward at the end of it all. It's sick.

RIMMER: Well, at least he's got twenty-four hours' notice. That's more than most of us get. All most of us get is mind that bus, what bus, splat! How's he taking it?

LISTER: He doesn't seem to be bothered. That's what narks me. He's just carried on doing his smegging duties. 25

RIMMER: Maybe I should talk to him. Maybe he needs a bit of counselling.

LISTER: You?

RIMMER: I used to work for the Samaritans.

LISTER: Yeah, for one morning.

RIMMER: Well, I couldn't take any more.

LISTER: I'm not surprised. You spoke to five people and they all committed suicide. I wouldn't mind, but one of them was a wrong number. He only phoned for the cricket scores.

RIMMER: It's hardly my fault that everyone picked that particular day to throw themselves off buildings. It made the papers: Lemming Sunday they called it.

LISTER: Maybe we can find his shut-down disk and turn it off, somehow.

RIMMER: He's not a kit droid. He's not like that stupid thing Petersen bought on Callisto. We wouldn't know where to begin.

LISTER: Yeah. You're right.

RIMMER: Come on – he's happy enough. You said yourself he's taking solace in his beliefs.

LISTER: Yeah, but his beliefs are a load of baloney.

26   RIMMER: Everyone's entitled to their beliefs. I

never agreed with my parents' religion, but I wouldn't dream of knocking it.

LISTER: What were they?

RIMMER: Seventh Day Advent Hoppists. They believed you had to spend every Sunday hopping. They'd hop down to church, hop through the service and hop back home again.

LISTER: What's the idea behind that, then?

RIMMER: Well, they took the Bible literally: Adam and Eve, the snake and the apple, took it word for word. Unfortunately their version had a misprint. It was all based on I Corinthians 13, where it says: 'Faith, Hop and Charity, and the greatest of these is Hop.' So that's what they used to do, every seventh day. I tell you, Sunday lunches were a nightmare. Hopping round the table, serving soup. We all had to wear sou'westers and asbestos underpants.

LISTER: The point is: what are we going to do about Kryten?

RIMMER: What can we do? He's pre-programed to self-destruct. Nothing we can say or do can stop it.

LISTER: Well, there's one thing we can do. At least we can make sure he goes out with a bang. We can give him the best smegging night of his life.

RIMMER: How do we do that? He doesn't like doing anything. His idea of a good time would be for us all to go up to the laundry room and fold some sheets. (*Mimics Kryten.*) 'Fun? Ah, yes: the employment of time in a profitless and non-practical way.'

LISTER: Hey – I'm not good at much, but the one thing I do know is how to lay on a good time.

Emohawk

Season Six.

Still stranded in Starbug, still searching for Red Dwarf, Rimmer tries to maintain discipline on board by holding regular drills . . .

1. Int. Cockpit

RIMMER *and* KRYTEN *at their stations. The red alert light is flashing.* CAT *and* LISTER *step up.*

RIMMER: Well, gentlemen, congratulations. Scrambling in a red alert situation, a new record time: one hour, seventeen minutes and thirty-nine seconds.

LISTER: Hey, not bad. And I bet we could get it down to one sixteen if we cut out that fourth round of toast.

CAT: One fifteen if we had it without Marmite.

RIMMER: You think I'm a petty-minded, bureaucratic nincompoop, who delights in enforcing 29 pernickety regulations because he gets some sort of perverse pleasure out of it. And in many ways, you're absolutely damned right. But that doesn't alter the fact that the only way we're going to track down Red Dwarf and get through this in one piece is with a sense of discipline, a sense of purpose and, wherever possible, a sensible haircut.

LISTER: I'm going back to bed.

RIMMER: I know it always draws great snickers of derision, but I repeat, self-discipline and short haircuts maketh man. Would it hurt you to have hair like mine?

CAT: I have got hair like yours. Just not on my head.

RIMMER: Well, I'm no stranger to the land of Scoff. But perhaps you'd like to explain, why it is that every major battle in history was won by the side with the shortest haircut?

KRYTEN: Oh, surely not, sir.

RIMMER: Think about it. Why did the US Cavalry beat the Indian nation? Short back and sides versus girlie hippie locks. The Round Heads and the Cavaliers? One nil to the pudding basins. Vietnam? Crew-cuts both sides, no score draw.

KRYTEN: Oh for a really world-class psychiatrist.

LISTER: All right, OK. What about Napoleon? He had short hair. So what happened at Waterloo?

RIMMER: Before the battle, he'd been on the march for a hundred days, and he sadly neglected my cardinal rule: an army marches on its haircut. On the eve of the battle the French forces looked like auditionees for a 1960s nude musical.

KRYTEN: Sir, that is preposterous. Napoleon's defeat was due to the unexpected late arrival of the Prussian forces.

RIMMER: Oh was it?

KRYTEN: Yes it was, sir.

RIMMER: And where had they been, these Prussian forces?

LISTER: Oh, for God's sake.

RIMMER: There's no evidence, I admit, but my bet? They all stopped off at Eine Cutten Uber Die Resten, for a quick cut-and-blow and a brief chat about where they were all going on holiday.

LISTER: Fascinating theory, man. You should write it down sometime with one of your non-toxic orange crayons, and try and get it published. I bet the *British Journal of Demented Delusions*'d snap it up.

RIMMER: Water off my back, Listy. Some of the greatest minds in history have been sneered and scoffed at.

LISTER: So have some of the biggest idiots.

CAT: Check your screens. I'm getting something up my left nostril, and it's coming in fast.

KRYTEN: Scans are all negative, sir. At the risk of challenging your olfactory excellence, perhaps a re-smelling is in order.

CAT: I'm telling you, Bud, my nostril hairs are shimmying faster than a grass skirt on a fat Hawaiian hoola-hoop champion. There's something out there.

KRYTEN: Screens clear. Sonar clear.

CAT: I say hit the re-heat and peel right.

LISTER: You heard him. Let's go.

RIMMER: I'm sick and tired of basing our whole navigational strategy on one feline's nose. I mean, I'm as much a fan of his right nostril as anyone, but I've made no bones about my lack of faith in his left. It's unreliable and difficult to work with.

KRYTEN: Not unreliable, sir, it's just the left nostril is ruled more by passion and intuition than the hard logic which controls the right.

RIMMER: I still maintain we should have that nostril removed from active duty.

LISTER: Wait a minute – I'm getting something on both of my ears. It's called drivel. Rimmer, just can it.

CAT: The read-outs have got to have something by now. It's directly ahead.

KRYTEN: Scans still dry.

RIMMER: That's it. I'm invoking Space Corps directive 91237.

KRYTEN: 91237? But, sir, surely that's impossible without at least one live chicken and a Rabbi?

RIMMER: Forget it. Forget I was ever born.

KRYTEN: Sir, I'm very happy to perform the ceremony, but I'm absolutely bewildered as to how sacrificing poultry might clear up the screen problem . . .

LISTER: Getting something! Major power surge off the port bow!

LISTER *looks right, everyone else looks left.*

LISTER: (*Without moving.*) Starboard bow. I thought I was facing the other way.

Everyone looks right.

KRYTEN: He's right. Some kind of vessel. It appears to be uncloaking.

LISTER: He's too damn close. That power surge'll toss us around like we're a bead of sweat in an aerobic teacher's buttock cleavage.

CAT: We're deader than kipper ties.

KRYTEN: Hang on! Here it comes!

Blue light. They get tossed about. Emergency lighting.

RIMMER: Damage report.

CAT: Superficial. NaviComp's down, slight rupture in fuel pipe nine and somehow the pilot's headset's got jammed on the Country and Western channel.

CAT takes off headset and smashes it with a monkey wrench.

KRYTEN: Second wave coming.

They are hit again.

KRYTEN: What is he thinking of, warping so close to another vessel? Damned space hog.

34 RIMMER: Something's materializing.

2. Model shot
Sphere-shaped ship warps into existence.

3. Int. Cockpit
Light bulbs start exploding all around them.

RIMMER: My God, that's a Space Corps External Enforcement Vehicle.

CAT: What?

LISTER: It's the Space Filth.

KRYTEN: A computer-controlled enforcement probe, unmanned. It's scanning us now.

RIMMER: Well. We've got nothing to fear. We're fine, upstanding, law-abiding citizens.

KRYTEN: Then why is it in arrest mode, sir?

RIMMER: Well, 75 per cent of us are.

CAT: Incoming.

Over the speaker, we hear:

COMPUTER: (*VO*) Property Corps Space removing and equipment Corps Space damaging, ships Corps Space of series a looting with charged formally are you. Two stroke three beta five Vehicle Enforcement External Corps Space is this.

KRYTEN: The materialization must have scrambled its voice unit. It's making about as much sense as a Japanese VCR instruction manual.

COMPUTER: (*VO*) Plead you do how?

RIMMER: It's in reverse. How do you plead?

CAT: How do we plead to what?

KRYTEN: It's charging us with looting Space Corps derelicts.

LISTER: We don't loot Space Corps derelicts. We just hack our way in and swipe stuff we need.

RIMMER: Lister, if this ever goes to trial, I demand separate lawyers.

CAT: What's the penalty for this? 'Cause if it means wearing outfits with arrows on, I'm committing suicide.

KRYTEN: No, it means wearing outfits with wings and haloes on, sir. The penalty is execution.

RIMMER: Why so harsh?

KRYTEN: It's frontier law, sir, and we are the deep space equivalent of horse rustlers. Severe sentencing is the only way to maintain order. Don't expect it to show us any mercy.

RIMMER: What do we do?

KRYTEN: Let's face it, sir: we're as guilty as the man behind the grassy knoll.

LISTER: But if we admit it, it'll blow us out of the stars.

RIMMER: Recommendations?

KRYTEN: Suggest I take the rap for everyone, sir. You can say I held you hostage, and forced you at gunpoint to do my evil bidding.

RIMMER: For God's sake, Kryten, we can't let you do that.

KRYTEN: Really?

RIMMER: Dream on, metal trash. Get your hands in the air and step into that searchlight.

CAT: There's an old Cat saying: 'If you lose a good friend, you can get another, but if you lose your tail, things will always be draughty.'

LISTER: That's about as clear as my bath water. What are you saying?

CAT: I'm saying, if you hand over your tail, sooner or later, you're gonna end up with whistle butt.

RIMMER: I swear, if you drilled three holes in his skull and blew through his ear, you could turn his head into an aboriginal hunting horn.

COMPUTER: (*VO*) Minute one have you.

KRYTEN: A thought occurs: if the orb's speech chip is reversed, there is every good chance that its logic chip is reversed also.

37

LISTER: Meaning?

KRYTEN: If we plead not guilty, the computer will think we're pleading guilty.

LISTER: But wait a minute: don't we *want* to convince it we're guilty? If we can prove we did the looting, because of its warped logic, the computer's got to find us innocent.

KRYTEN: Good thinking, sir. On the other hand if it finds us innocent, its reversed thought processes will force it to punish us. Whereas, if it finds us guilty, in its twisted thinking, it will let us walk free.

RIMMER: So where does that leave us?

KRYTEN: I'm saying: with all its warped and reversed logics, our one chance of getting off this thing is to plead not guilty, and then prove our innocence. It's the only way to beat that insane machine.

RIMMER: Rolls-Royce logic, Kryten. The only micron-sized blemish on the Van Den Plaas finish of your reasoning is, we are guilty. We have looted derelicts. We're nicked.

LISTER: No choices then. We leg it. Plot a course for Scarper City.

38   LISTER *flicks switches.*

KRYTEN: Sir, a class 'A' enforcement orb can out-run us easily.

LISTER: Kryten, a zimmer-frame relay team can outrun us easily. It's not about speed, it's about wit, brains and cunning.

KRYTEN: I was praying it wouldn't come to that, sir.

LISTER: Take a look at your screens. We're seven klicks away from the GELF *zone*. *It wouldn't follow us in there in a gazillion years.*

RIMMER: No. Because GELFs are untrustworthy scavengers, with no regard for law, life or property.

LISTER: Right. So we'll be safe.

RIMMER: Lister, you've heard the stories. They skin humans alive and turn them into beanbags. Unless you want a triple-buttocked GELF sitting on your face for the rest of eternity, probing your crevices for lost forks and biros, I suggest you rethink.

KRYTEN: It's the lesser of two evils, sir. In the absence of a sane plan, I suggest we go with Mr Lister's.

CAT: You want to know what I think?

ALL: No.

39

LISTER: OK, Cat, on my mark, re-heat, hard a-starboard.

LISTER *looks left. Everyone else looks right.*

LISTER: (*Without moving.*) Port. Has somebody been moving my chair?

Everyone looks left.

COMPUTER: (*VO*) Seconds twenty in firing commence in will I reply a of absence in.

LISTER: Roughly translated: hit the re-heat.

CAT: You don't have to tell me twice.

Long uncomfortable pause. CAT *does nothing.*

LISTER: Cat, man. Hit the re-heat.

CAT: Sorry, Bud, looks like you *do* have to tell me twice.

CAT *hits the re-heat and they accelerate off.*

Timeslides

Season Three.

After the crew discover some mutated developing liquid which allows them to enter old photographs, Lister goes back into his past to give his younger self some advice on how to get seriously rich.

1. Int. Pub

YOUNG LISTER *is on the stage, singing.*

YOUNG LISTER: (*Singing*) Omm . . . omm . . . ommm . . .

LISTER *stands watching him.* CAT, KRYTEN *and* RIMMER *appear.*

LISTER: That was one of the first songs I ever wrote. It was called 'Om'.

CAT: No kidding.

RIMMER: Nothing like a good, old-fashioned love song.

LISTER: And to think: I genuinely thought we were going to make it. God, I was stupid.

RIMMER: Who are the other two?

LISTER: The whacked-out crazy hippy drummer's called 'Dobbin'.

We see the DRUMMER. *A completely whacked-out crazy hippy, smacking the drums with a fag in his mouth.*

LISTER: He joined the police force in the end. Became a grand Wizard in the Freemasons. The bassist is Gary. He was a neo-Marxist-nihilistic anarchist. Eventually, he joined a large insurance company and got his own parking space.

The music finishes. There is a smattering of disguised applause from the band themselves.

YOUNG LISTER: (*Into feedbacky mic*) Thank you. Thank you very much. For those of you who are interested, there are some official Smeg-and-the-Heads T-shirts, and some signed polaroids of the band, currently on sale in the back of Dobbin's car. It's the orange Ford in the carpark, the one with bald tyres and no windscreen. Well, we'll be back with our second set in twenty minutes. So from me, Smeg, and from Dobbin and Gary, the Heads, see you later.

YOUNG LISTER *steps down from the stage.* LISTER *goes over to him. The others sit down at a table.*

KRYTEN: What is this place?

RIMMER: It's a pub.

KRYTEN: Pub. Ah, yes. A meeting-place where people attempt to achieve advanced states of mental incompetence by the repeated consumption of fermented vegetable drinks.

LISTER: Guys – I'd like you to meet me aged seventeen.

YOUNG LISTER: Shady. This is just totally shady. It's beyond shady. It's surreal. Are these your mates, then?

LISTER: Cat, Kryten, Rimmer.

YOUNG LISTER: (*To* RIMMER) Brutal tattoo man. (*Indicates* RIMMER's 'H'.) What's it stand for? 'Heavy metal'?

RIMMER: I beg your pardon?

YOUNG LISTER: And what's happened to him? (*Points at* KRYTEN) His face – it's grotesque, innit? Has he had an accident? He looks like he spent three weeks with his head jammed in a lift. Brutal. Shady. Surreal, eh?

LISTER: Sit down, and shut up.

YOUNG LISTER: So – how've you got here? What d'you want?

LISTER: I've come to try and change our future.

YOUNG LISTER: Change it? Aren't you happy being a rock star, then? Are the constant demands of the groupies getting you down?

LISTER: We don't make it as a rock star.

YOUNG LISTER: You what? That's just totally not possible. It cannot be. We're already nearly sort of nearly semi-pro at the moment, and we've almost got a definite guarantee of probably getting a recording contract, possibly. How can we fail?

LISTER: How can I say this without giving offence? The reason you don't make it is because ... you're crap.

YOUNG LISTER: What do you know, grandad? You're too old to receive what we're trying to transmit.

LISTER: I'm you, you dork.

YOUNG LISTER: Too old, and too crypto-fascist.

44 LISTER: Will you shut up and listen to me? I'm

going to give you something that's going to make you rich. All you've got to do is take it to the Patent Office and get it registered as your invention. It's called a tension sheet.

LISTER *takes the tension sheet out of his pocket and hands it over to* YOUNG LISTER.

RIMMER: Uh-huh-huh – that's immoral! That's Thickie Holden's invention.

LISTER: Uh-huh-huh – Was.

YOUNG LISTER: This is just the stuff they use as packing paper. Painted red. With 'tension sheet' printed on it.

LISTER: I know.

YOUNG LISTER: It's a piece of crypto-fascist, bourgeois crap.

LISTER: It will make you a multi-multi-millionaire.

YOUNG LISTER: But I'm not into dosh. I hate money. I loathe possessions. It's just so crypto-fascist.

LISTER: Will you stop saying everything's crypto-fascist? You're making me sound like I was a complete git.

YOUNG LISTER: Look – I'm not breaking up the band. Music is my life.

RIMMER: He's right – you can't make him give up his music. You heard the 'om' song. It's a masterpiece.

YOUNG LISTER: See?

LISTER: (*To* RIMMER) Keep out of this. (*To* YOUNG LISTER) I'm trying to give you a break.

CAT: Oh, give up. The guy's an idiot.

LISTER: He's me.

CAT: Like I say, the guy's an idiot.

YOUNG LISTER: I don't want a break. It's my future. I'll take my own chances.

LISTER: If you take your own chances, you'll wind up stuck on a spaceship with these three for the rest of eternity. You won't have any future. Think about it.

LISTER *stands.*

LISTER: Come on.

CAT, KRYTEN *and* RIMMER *follow* LISTER *out of the photograph. Before he leaves,* RIMMER *turns to* YOUNG LISTER.

RIMMER: Er, you haven't got a copy of that 'om' song I could take back with me, have you?

YOUNG LISTER: They're all in the car.

RIMMER: Pity. I just can't get it out of my head. So catchy. (*Sings*) 'Omm'. Keep writing those hits, kid.

Holoship

'Holoship' was the opening show in Season Five. At the recording, the show overran by ten minutes, and the broadcast version had to be cut quite dramatically. The following sequence was never transmitted in its entirety.

The crew have encountered a strange vessel, the Enlightenment, peopled entirely by 'holograms of great genius and bravery'. Holocrews are 'legendarily arrogant', enjoying superior IQs, and attitudes vastly different from the Red Dwarf crew's.

Rimmer has been transported aboard the holoship, where he meets the beautiful Nirvana Crane . . .

1. Int. Lift. Holoship. Day

RIMMER *and* NIRVANA *are in a futuristic lift – strip lights up the side indicate lift movement.*

LIFT: Floor 124 Maintenance Department . . .
RIMMER: . . . But what's your mission?
NIRVANA: Exploration. We trawl deep space, in

48

search of new life-forms, and unique physical phenomena.

RIMMER: Fascinating. How big's the crew?

NIRVANA: Just under two thousand. All top-flight personnel.

RIMMER: What a ship! What a magnificent vessel!

LIFT: Floor 125 – Sports and Sexual Recreation.

RIMMER: Sports and what?

NIRVANA: Sex. Don't you have a Sex Deck on your ship?

RIMMER: No.

NIRVANA: Well, what do you do when you want to have sex?

RIMMER: Well, we go for runs . . . watch gardening programmes on the ship's vid . . . play blow football . . . lots of things.

NIRVANA: That's . . . very bad for you. Don't you ever feel tense and frustrated?

RIMMER: Well, it's got worse these last ten years or so, I can't deny it. But uh . . .

NIRVANA: Extraordinary. It's quite different here. In fact it's a ship regulation that we all make love at least twice a day. It's a health rule.

RIMMER: Twice a day? That's more than some people manage in a lifetime!

He catches her expression — puzzled.

RIMMER: I mean, sad people. Sad, sad, lonely people. (*Beat.*) Whu ... what happens if you don't have a partner?

NIRVANA: (*Not understanding.*) If you don't have a partner?

RIMMER: I mean, some people ... find that they're just ... that people ... that people just aren't attracted to them in ... in that way.

NIRVANA: I don't understand. Here, it's considered the height of bad manners to refuse an offer of sexual coupling.

RIMMER: (*Pause.*) Well ... people have always complimented me on my good manners ... What a ship!

NIRVANA: We discarded the concept of Family in the twenty-fifth century, when scientists finally proved that all our hang-ups and neuroses are caused by our parents.

RIMMER: I knew it!

NIRVANA: Families are disastrous for your mental health. So are relationships. These are outmoded concepts for us.

RIMMER: What about love? I mean, surely people still fall in love?

NIRVANA: We have developed beyond 'love,' Mr
    Rimmer. It is a short-term hormonal distraction
    which interferes with the pure pursuit of personal
    advancement. We are holograms: there is no risk of
    disease or pregnancy. That's why, in our society,
    we believe only in sex. Constant, guilt-free sex.
RIMMER: Well, Nirvana, I always say: when in
    Rome . . . wear a toga.

Lift stops.

LIFT: Deck 177. Senior Officers' Quarters.
NIRVANA: Our floor. Come on, meet the Captain.
    Then if there's time, we'll grab some supper and
    have sex.

She walks out of the lift, leaving RIMMER *temporarily
stunned. He gathers himself together.*

RIMMER: Oh, that would be lovely. (*Starts to follow
    her, out of shot.*) Yes, lovely . . .

2. Int. Nirvana's quarters. Moody

RIMMER *and* NIRVANA *are lying post-coitally under
silk sheets.*

RIMMER: That was just . . . unbelievable. 51

NIRVANA: Nobody's ever made love to me like that before.

RIMMER: Was it OK?

NIRVANA: It was . . . different.

RIMMER: Different?

NIRVANA: It had such . . . gusto.

RIMMER: It's probably coming from a large family. At mealtimes we always had to eat as fast as we could so we could get back for seconds.

NIRVANA: You make love like a Japanese meal — small portions, but so many courses.

RIMMER: Listen. I'm not very good at this sort of thing, but I just want to say . . . I think you are the most beautiful woman I've ever seen who didn't have staples through her stomach. Really, you're gorgeous, I mean, I'm constantly fighting the urge to fold you in thirds. Oh, God, what am I saying? Someone stop me. I'm trying to say you are incredibly incredible.

NIRVANA: That's not our way. We don't pay compliments. This is just . . . exercise. Nothing more.

RIMMER: That's all it is to me, too. Exercise. It's just . . . I've never worked out with such fantastic gym equipment.

NIRVANA: Emotion distracts the mind from the pursuit of intellectual excellence. We must dress and go now.

RIMMER: Look, Nirvana, what I'm trying to say is . . .

NIRVANA: Please don't say anything.

They both swing their legs over the edge of the bed (they are both in long T-shirts) so they are facing away from each other.

RIMMER: Look – I hope you didn't get the wrong idea, back there. It meant nothing to me. Really. Less than nothing. Truly.

NIRVANA: Good.

RIMMER: We might as well have been playing tennis.

NIRVANA: As it should be.

RIMMER: I, uh, I don't suppose you fancy a tie-break?

NIRVANA: I'm sorry. I've got things I should do.

RIMMER: *Niet problemski.*

Pregnant pause.

NIRVANA: You know, usually, we talk.

RIMMER: Talk?

NIRVANA: During the exercise.

RIMMER: What do you talk about?

NIRVANA: Ohh . . . research . . . new theories . . . mission profiles . . .

RIMMER: I'm sorry. I must have seemed very rude. I hardly said anything. Apart from 'Geronimo'.

She shakes his hand.

NIRVANA: Thank you for the workout.

RIMMER: And thank you for what must rate as the weirdest afternoon of my life.

RIMMER *vanishes.*

Kryten

Season Two.

This is the show that introduced Kryten.

Holly receives a distress signal from a crashed vessel, Nova 5. Responding to the SOS, the crew contact the Nova 5's mechanoid, Kryten, who begs them to land and rescue his injured crew, comprising three women.

The prospect of contacting live human females after three million years without female company sends the on-board testosterone count off the scale. The crew prepare for the rescue . . .

1. Int. Sleeping quarters. Day

LISTER *is getting ready to go out on the pull, grooving along to his ghetto-blaster as he prepares his clothes. He is wearing off-white boxer shorts. His trousers are on the ironing board. He is buffing his shoes with a cloth. Spit and buff. He's really doing a good job on these shoes. He finishes, then puts on the polishing cloth – it's his T-shirt. He grooves over to his locker and pulls out his single remaining clean sock. He tuts, bops*

*over to the laundry basket and pulls out a very stiff,
very smelly orange sock. He holds it at arm's length
and sprays it with deodorant. He puts it on the ironing
board and hits it several times with a toffee hammer.
He grooves over to the sink, picks up the toothpaste
with his right hand, tosses it over to his left, picks up
his toothbrush, squirts the paste in the air and starts
brushing. He crosses to the ironing board, picks up his
trousers and puts them on. The iron has burnt a hole
clean through to the right cheek. He grooves over to
the locker, takes out a can of black spray paint and
sprays the corresponding part of his boxer shorts.*

LISTER: Perfection.

RIMMER *comes in, sporting his dashing white official
uniform, complete with his medals.*

RIMMER: Oh. You're not on the pull? Look at
you: it's pathetic. You're wearing all your least
smeggy things.

LISTER: Don't know what you're talking about.

RIMMER: That T-shirt with only the two curry
stains on it: you only wear that on special
occasions. You're toffed up to the nines.

56 LISTER: What about you? You look like Clive of India.

RIMMER: Oh, it's started. I knew it would.

LISTER: What has?

RIMMER: The put-downs. Always the same, when-ever we meet girls. Put me down, and make yourself look good.

LISTER: Like when?

RIMMER: Remember those two little brunettes from Supplies? And I told them I worked in the stores, and they were very interested and asked me what I did there . . .

LISTER: And I said you were a shelf.

RIMMER: Right. And when I suggested a little trip to Titan zoo, you said: 'Oooh, he's taking you home to see his mum already.'

LISTER: So? They laughed.

RIMMER: Yes. At me. At my expense. Just don't put me down when we meet them.

LISTER: How d'you want me to act?

RIMMER: Just show a little respect. For a start, don't call me 'Rimmer'.

LISTER: Why not?

RIMMER: Because you always hit the '*Rim*' at the beginning. *Rim*mer. You make it sound like a lavatory disinfectant.

LISTER: Well, what should I call you? Rim*mer*?

RIMMER: I dunno. Arnie. Or Arn. Something a bit more . . . I dunno. How about Big Man?

LISTER: Big Man??

RIMMER: Or the nickname I had at school.

LISTER: Bonehead?

RIMMER: How did you know my nickname was Bonehead?

LISTER: I just guessed.

RIMMER: Well, I didn't mean that one. I meant the other one.

LISTER: Which one?

RIMMER: Ace.

LISTER: Your nickname was never Ace. Maybe Ace-hole.

RIMMER: It was my nickname, actually. It's just, nobody ever called it me, no matter how many times I let them beat me up. I'm just saying: don't knock me down. Build me up.

LISTER: Like?

RIMMER: Like, if the chance occurs, and it comes up naturally in the conversation, perhaps you could mention I'm very brave.

LISTER: Do what?

RIMMER: Don't go ape. Just, you know, perhaps, when my back's turned, you could mention that

I died, and I was, well, pretty incredibly brave about it.

LISTER *stares at him.*

RIMMER: Or . . . just kind of hint that I've had quite a few girlfriends.

LISTER *stares.*

RIMMER: Fine. Forget it. Just an idea. You're not wearing those boots, are you?

LISTER: Why? What's wrong with them?

RIMMER: They don't go. Not with that outfit. You should wear those dayglo orange moon boots.

LISTER: Eh? You said they were disgusting.

RIMMER: No. Very chic.

LISTER: You said they smelled like an orang-utan's posing pouch. You made me put them in the airlock.

RIMMER: No. They look terrific on you. I'd wear 'em.

LISTER: Honest?

RIMMER: Definitely.

2. Int. Nova 5 corridor. Dim

KRYTEN *is rushing down the sloping corridor.*

KRYTEN: Come on! They're here, everybody.
They're in orbit. Heavens! There's so much to
do.

He pauses to water a plant, and carries on.

3. Int. Nova 5 service deck. Day

KRYTEN *scurries in. Seated around the table are*
THREE SKELETONS WITH LONG HAIR, *in Nova*
5 uniforms.

KRYTEN: Miss Jane! You haven't brushed your hair!

KRYTEN *starts combing a* SKELETON*'s hair.*

KRYTEN: What a mess you look.

He takes out some lipstick and applies it to the
SKELETON.

KRYTEN: And Miss Anne – why haven't you
touched your soup? It's no wonder you've started
looking so pasty.

There is a creak, and Miss Anne's SKELETON *slumps*
head first into her soup.

60 KRYTEN: Eat nicely, Miss Anne. What on Earth

will the visitors think if they see you eating like that?

He goes up to the blonde SKELETON *brandishing his hairbrush.*

KRYTEN: Now then, Miss Tracy . . . (*Hesitates.*) No, you look absolutely perfect.

4. Int. Blue Midget. Space

Pan up from LISTER*'s vile orange moon boots.* RIMMER *is standing beside him, trying to pretend there's no stench.*

LISTER: (*Sniffs.*) What's that smell?
RIMMER: I can't smell anything.
LISTER: Are you OK? Your eyes are watering.
RIMMER: Excitement. Look, we can't wait for the Cat. Let's just go.
LISTER: Come on: he's been preparing for a day and a night. Don't you want to see the result?

The CAT *comes in. He is wearing a gold space suit, like Armani would design, with a helmet two feet high and cone-shaped.*

CAT: I am a plastic surgeon's nightmare! Throw

the scalpel away: improvements are impossible!

RIMMER: A space suit with cuff-links?

LISTER: Where'd you get that helmet?

CAT: Made it myself. Didn't want to muss up my hair. We just got to make sure we don't pass any mirrors, 'cause if we do, I'm there for the day.

HOLLY *appears on the monitor, wearing a toupee.*

HOLLY: All right? Everybody ready? Let's go, then.

LISTER: Holly, man: what are you doing?

HOLLY: What's wrong?

LISTER: The rug. Why are you wearing a toupee?

HOLLY: What toupee?

LISTER: The one on your head.

HOLLY: Whose head, then?

LISTER: Your head. You look like a game-show host.

HOLLY: Oh. So it's not undetectable then. It doesn't blend in naturally and seamlessly with my own natural hair?

RIMMER: What is wrong with everybody? Three million years without a woman, and you all act like you're fourteen years old.

62 HOLLY: Oh, yeah? What about you and the socks?

LISTER: What socks?

RIMMER: Well, come on. We can't hang around . . .

HOLLY: He wanted two pairs of socks.

CAT: What for?

HOLLY: One pair to put on his feet, the other pair to roll up and put down his trousers.

RIMMER *crosses his legs.*

5. Int. Nova 5 corridor. Day

KRYTEN *opens the airlock, and* LISTER, RIMMER *and the* CAT *step in.*

KRYTEN: Come in, come in. How lovely to meet you.

RIMMER: *Cârmita!* What a delightful craft. Reminds me of my first command.

KRYTEN: This way.

RIMMER *mouths to* LISTER: *'Ace, Ace'.* LISTER *pretends not to understand. They follow* KRYTEN. *They pass a mirror. The* CAT *catches sight of himself and freezes.*

CAT: You're a work of art, baby.

LISTER: Come on.

CAT: You're gonna have to help me.

LISTER *drags at* CAT, *who clings on to the mirror until he's torn away.*

CAT: Thanks, Bud.

KRYTEN: I'm so excited. We all are. The girls could hardly stop themselves from jumping up and down.

RIMMER: (*Brays falsely*) Oh, cârmita, cârmita.

KRYTEN: *Ah! Vi parolas esperanton, Kapitano Rimmer?*

RIMMER: Come again?

KRYTEN: You speak Esperanto, Captain Rimmer?

RIMMER: Oh, *si si si. Jawol. Oui.*

6. Int. Nova 5 service deck. Day
The SKELETONS, *as before.* KRYTEN *enters.*

KRYTEN: Well, here they are.

RIMMER *comes in, and bows deeply.*

RIMMER: *Cârmita!*

He looks up. LISTER *and the* CAT *come in behind him. A long pause, as they all take in the view.*

LISTER: Well. It's difficult to know what to say, isn't it, Ace?

KRYTEN: Well, isn't anybody going to say 'hello'?

LISTER: I think that little blonde one's giving you the eye.

KRYTEN: Now, you all get to know one another. I'll go and fetch some tea.

KRYTEN *waddles off. The* CAT *sits next to one of the* SKELETONS.

CAT: Hi, baby. What's happening? Did anyone ever tell you you have lovely eye sockets? Let's jump in a hot tub, we could make great soup together.

RIMMER: I don't believe this.

LISTER: Be strong, Big Man.

RIMMER: Our one contact with intelligent life in three million and two years, and he's the android equivalent of Norman Bates.

CAT: Come on, guys. So they're a little on the skinny side.

LISTER: I know this may not be the time or the place to say this, but Ace here is incredibly brave.

RIMMER: Smeg off, dogfood face.

LISTER: And he's got just tons of girlfriends. 65

RIMMER: I'm warning you, Lister.

KRYTEN *returns with a tea-tray*.

KRYTEN: Is there something wrong?
RIMMER: Something wrong? They're dead.
KRYTEN: Who's dead?
RIMMER: (*Nods at skeletons*.) *They're* dead. They're all dead.
KRYTEN: My God. I was only away two minutes.
RIMMER: They've been dead for centuries.
KRYTEN: No.
RIMMER: Yes.
KRYTEN: Are you a doctor?
RIMMER: You only have to look at them. They've got less meat on them than a chicken nugget!
KRYTEN: But what will I do? I'm programed to serve them.
LISTER: Well, first thing, we should bury them.
KRYTEN: You're *that* sure they're dead?
RIMMER: Yes!

KRYTEN *goes over to the blonde* SKELETON.

KRYTEN: What about this one?
RIMMER: Well, there's a simple test. All right, girls. Hands up if you're alive.

KRYTEN *urges the* SKELETONS *to react. He is crest-fallen when they do not.*

KRYTEN: What am I to do?

LISTER: You've got to start a new life now.

KRYTEN: I don't have the software to cope with this. I was created to serve. I serve, therefore I am. That is my purpose: to serve and have no regard for myself.

LISTER: Well, you've got to change. You've got to work out what you want, Kryten, and stop being everybody's smegging doormat.

KRYTEN: That's easy for you to say. You're a human.

RIMMER: Only just.

Out of Time

'Out of Time' was the final show in Season Six.

Again, this is the opening scene. Rimmer is now a 'hard light' hologram – he can touch things

1. Int. Mid-section

KRYTEN, CAT *and* LISTER *having coffee at the scanner table.* RIMMER *comes down the ops room steps, and crosses to the scanner. There is an air of new adulthood and maturity about him.*

RIMMER: Gentlemen, thank you for attending this meeting. Let me begin by saying, it can't have escaped anyone's attention that things have been getting pretty strained around here of late, and I felt it was high time we all sat round and tried to address some of the problems. It's no secret that morale's on the floor – we've lost all trace of Red Dwarf, supplies are low, tempers are strained. So if no one objects, I've appointed myself morale officer and set myself the task of

trying to raise spirits and improve the atmos-
phere all round.

ALL *look a bit impressed.*

RIMMER: To kick off, I thought that, once a week,
it might be productive for us all to come together,
have a coffee, beer, whatever's your poison, and
get any problems you may have off your chests.
Any objec tions?
ALL:(*Mumble ad lib*) No. Sure. Whatever.
RIMMER: Why don't I start? You know what really
makes me puke about Lister? You know what
really makes me want to stab him in both eyes
with an ice-pick? Everything, that's what, especially his God-awful chirpy, gerbil-faced optimism. And as for the Cat? I mean, what an
unbelievable git! And Kryten. If he doesn't
change pronto, I swear I'll attach jump leads to
his nipple nuts and fry him like a Cajun catfish.
(*Suddenly calm.*) Well, excellent, that's really
cleared the air. I for one certainly feel much
better. Thanks for your contributions, gentlemen
– see you all at the next morale meeting a week
today. Marvellous.

RIMMER *gets up and goes back to the ops room.*

LISTER: Good meeting.

CAT: What's eating him?

KRYTEN: Well, I'm no psychologist, sir, but maybe the bleak, lonely, pointless emptiness of our hopeless, futile predicament is beginning to get him down.

CAT: You can always tell when he's tense. The way he scrunches up cups and throws them in the bin. And we're not talking Styrofoam here, we're talking enamel.

LISTER: I told you, didn't I, that he attacked me with that fridge?

KRYTEN: What happened?

LISTER: He just wrenched it off the wall and tried to insert it in me.

KRYTEN: What did you do to upset him?

LISTER: Absolutely nothing. I was just sitting there, minding my own business, plucking out my lengthier nostril hairs with a pair of cooking tongs.

KRYTEN: Extraordinary. So unprovoked.

CAT: Guy's so touchy. If *I* tried to force-feed you a refrigerator every time you did something gross, you'd have to go on a fridge diet.

LISTER: You know what the problem is? Every day's the same old slog through deep space. No variety. Take Christmas. What did we do Christmas Day?

KRYTEN: Well, if you remember, sir, Christmas Day we were attacked by that pan-dimensional liquid beast from the Mogadon Cluster.

LISTER: Maybe that wasn't such a great example, then. I'm trying to say: our lives are dull. Repetitive. We never take time out to smell the roses. We never celebrate anything.

CAT: We've got nothing to celebrate with, Bud.

KRYTEN: Not true, sir. There's a whole case of that wine I brewed out of urine recyc just lying there practically untouched.

LISTER: Call me pretentious if you like, but for me, a truly great wine should not leave you with a foam moustache that you can only remove with turps.

CAT: (*Sniffs.*) Strange.

LISTER: What is it?

CAT: I'm getting something. Trouble.

SFX: low-volume warning sound.

KRYTEN: You're absolutely correct, sir. Autopilot alert.

As RIMMER *comes down the stairs,* LISTER, CAT *and* KRYTEN *rush up into cockpit.*

2. Int. Cockpit

LISTER, CAT, KRYTEN *and* RIMMER *take up their stations.*

CAT: Storm front ahead. Switching to manual.

LISTER: It's a big one – too late to go round, it's right on us.

KRYTEN: Stellar fog. Tightly packed particles from an exploded supernova. Our scanners won't be able to penetrate more than a few metres.

CAT: Slowing to minimum.

RIMMER: Gentlemen, absolute concentration till we're through the squall. There could be anything lurking in there.

CAT: Don't worry, Bud. If there's anything out there, we'll spot it.

Huge collision. Light change. LISTER *is flung from his seat.*

RIMMER: Anybody hurt?

CAT: Well, my pride sure needs mouth-to-mouth.

KRYTEN: Mr Lister, sir! He's out cold.

CAT: All stop. Let's get him up to the Ops room.

3. Int. Ops room

LISTER *on the medibed, his left arm bloody and injured.* CAT *and* RIMMER *look on as* KRYTEN *examines him.*

RIMMER: How is he?
KRYTEN: Not good, sir.

KRYTEN *cuts away Lister's sleeve.*

KRYTEN: (*To* RIMMER) Sir, this is getting a little messy, perhaps you'd better look away – I know you can't stand the sight of blood.
RIMMER: Don't worry, Kryten, I'm OK when it's Lister's.
KRYTEN: (*Astonished.*) Not possible.
CAT: What?
KRYTEN: Look.

Shot: Lister's arm. A flap of skin is folded back, revealing a robotic endoskeleton inside.

KRYTEN: Mr Lister is a droid.
RIMMER: He's a what?

KRYTEN: No doubt about it. He is entirely mechanical. A three thousand series. Made in Taiwan. Look – here's a 24-hour emergency call-out number.

RIMMER: I'm sorry, I am not buying this. Who'd create him? And why? What's his mission? To rid the Universe of chicken vindaloo?

CAT: This doesn't tie up. If he wasn't human, I'd have known from his scent.

KRYTEN *produces X-ray of robot.*

KRYTEN: The X-rays confirm it. This is so strange. Mr Lister's always been an icon of mine, and now I find he's an earlier model, and technically, I outrank him.

RIMMER: Earlier model – but then why does he look so much more sophisticated than you?

KRYTEN: Sir, just because I have a head shaped like a freak formation of mashed potato, does not mean I am unsophisticated.

RIMMER: All right then, why does he look more realistically human?

KRYTEN: Humans have always found exact duplicates rather disturbing, sir. The three thousand series was notoriously unpopular. Most of them were recalled. A few slipped the net and went undercover to make new lives in society.

CAT: So you think he knows?

KRYTEN: Unlikely. He probably reprogramed his own memory to escape detection.

CAT: This is going to crack him up – devastate him. Who's gonna tell him?

RIMMER: I'll write you into my will if you let it be me.

LISTER *stirs*.

KRYTEN: Suggest you leave this to me, sirs. I'll have a talk with him, droid to droid.

RIMMER: OK. We'll get under way – try and get out of this damn fog before it drains the solar batteries.

CAT *and* RIMMER *exit*.

LISTER: (*Groans*) What happened? What hit us?

KRYTEN: Something in the stellar fog, sir. Didn't show up on the scans. Sir, do you remember who your parents were?

LISTER: You know I don't. I was found in a box under a pool table.

KRYTEN: Did anyone ever tell you what was

written on that box? I mean, were the words: 'Kit', or 'Paint before assembling' ever mentioned? It's just that, while you were under, we discovered something rather disturbing about you.

LISTER: It's that tattoo on my inner thigh, isn't it? Look, I don't really love Petersen, he just got me so drunk, I didn't know what I was doing.

KRYTEN: It's not the tattoo, sir. There's no easy way of breaking this gently.

KRYTEN *pulls back the loose dressing on Lister's arm.*

KRYTEN: I'm afraid, sir, you are not human. You're a droid.

LISTER: . . . I'm a what?

KRYTEN: You're a mechanical. Three thousand series. Technically subordinate to me.

LISTER: What does this all mean?

KRYTEN: Well, in broad terms, I get the front seat in the cockpit, and you're in charge of the laundry.

KRYTEN *hands* LISTER *laundry basket.*

KRYTEN: I want to see creases!

LISTER: Kryten, have a heart, man, I'm in gobsmack overload, here.

KRYTEN: You're a droid – you don't have real emotions – it's just synthi-shock. Now stop thinking like a human and go about your duties.

LISTER: Why are you being so heartless?

KRYTEN: I looked up to you. You encouraged me to break my programing and ape human behaviour. Now I find you're no better than I am. But worst of all, the most bitter pill to swallow, for four long years I had to hand-scrub the gussets on your long johns. Now, unless you want to wallow in the eternal fires of Silicon Hell I suggest you bring a tray of refreshments to the cockpit, pronto.

KRYTEN *turns to exit, there is another jolt, light change, everything shakes.*

4. Int. Cockpit

CAT *and* RIMMER *at their stations,* KRYTEN *steps in and takes Lister's seat.*

KRYTEN: What was the jolt?

CAT: It's a mystery, Bud. Nothing on the scanners, nothing on visual.

RIMMER: It's like we went through some kind of

energy pocket. Still, looks like we're out of it now.

KRYTEN: Better run a cross-check, see if this phenomenon is mentioned in any of our databases.

LISTER *steps through with a tea-tray, and offers it to the* CAT.

LISTER: (*Sheepish*) Tea up. Sorry I was so long, I didn't know where anything was.

KRYTEN: Let me see that tray, please.

LISTER: Why?

KRYTEN: That's: 'Why, Mr Kryten, sir?'

KRYTEN *examines the fayre.*

KRYTEN: Call those triangular sandwiches? Did you use a set square? I think not. And the chocolate finger display is laughable. Don't just pile them higgledy-piggledy on to a plate – make them into an attractive interlaced log-cabin structure, or something. This will just not do. Now kindly return to the galley, and start again.

LISTER: This really doesn't feel right. Not right at all.

LISTER *exits.*

RIMMER: What a charlatan! All these years.

CAT: Any idea what hit us yet?

KRYTEN *checks his screens.*

KRYTEN: Wait. Here's something. Reports of artificial stellar fogs which contain Reality Minefields.

CAT: Reality what?

KRYTEN: Bubbles or pockets of unreality, which, when encountered, create false realities designed to disorient and drive off potential looters.

RIMMER: From what?

KRYTEN: It's a defence device fitted to Space Corps test ships which are fitted with prototype drives so awesome in their power, they have to be safeguarded at all costs.

RIMMER: So we just crashed through an unreality pocket?

KRYTEN: Which created a false reality, making us believe Mr Lister was . . . Oh my.

CAT: You mean he's not a . . .

KRYTEN: Yes.

LISTER *steps up into the cockpit, with another tray.* 79

LISTER: Tea up, sirs.

KRYTEN: Sir, I . . .

LISTER *pulls off platter lid revealing an elaborate chocolate finger log cabin, complete with picket fence and a couple of plastic farm animals.*

LISTER: What d'you think? I'm not happy with the picket fence. I'll go and rebuild it if you want.

KRYTEN: Sir, may I see your arm?

LISTER *shows his arm.*

LISTER: Smeg. It looks normal now. Human.

KRYTEN: Someone else tell him. I've got gussets to scrub.

KRYTEN *exits.*

PENGUIN 60s

ISABEL ALLENDE · *Voices in My Ear*
NICHOLSON BAKER · *Playing Trombone*
LINDSEY BAREHAM · *The Little Book of Big Soups*
KAREN BLIXEN · *From the Ngong Hills*
DIRK BOGARDE · *Coming of Age*
ANTHONY BURGESS · *Childhood*
ANGELA CARTER · *Lizzie Borden*
CARLOS CASTANEDA · *The Sorcerer's Ring of Power*
ELIZABETH DAVID · *Peperonata and Other Italian Dishes*
RICHARD DAWKINS · *The Pocket Watchmaker*
GERALD DURRELL · *The Pageant of Fireflies*
RICHARD ELLMANN · *The Trial of Oscar Wilde*
EPICURUS · *Letter on Happiness*
MARIANNE FAITHFULL · *Year One*
KEITH FLOYD · *Hot and Spicy Floyd*
ALEXANDER FRATER · *Where the Dawn Comes Up like Thunder*
ESTHER FREUD · *Meeting Bilal*
JOHN KENNETH GALBRAITH · *The Culture of Contentment*
ROB GRANT AND DOUG NAYLOR · *Scenes from the Dwarf*
ROBERT GRAVES · *The Gods of Olympus*
JANE GRIGSON · *Puddings*
SOPHIE GRIGSON · *From Sophie's Table*
KATHARINE HEPBURN · *Little Me*
JAMES HERRIOT · *Seven Yorkshire Tales*
SUSAN HILL · *The Badness within Him*
ALAN HOLLINGHURST · *Adventures Underground*
BARRY HUMPHRIES · *Less is More Please*
HOWARD JACOBSON · *Expulsion from Paradise*
P. D. JAMES · *The Girl Who Loved Graveyards*
STEPHEN KING · *Umney's Last Case*

PENGUIN 60s

READ MORE IN PENGUIN

For complete information about books available from Penguin and how to order them, please write to us at the appropriate address below. Please note that for copyright reasons the selection of books varies from country to country.

IN THE UNITED KINGDOM: Please write to *Dept. EP, Penguin Books Ltd, Bath Road, Harmondsworth, Middlesex UB7 0DA.*

IN THE UNITED STATES: Please write to *Consumer Sales, Penguin USA, P.O. Box 999, Dept. 17109, Bergenfield, New Jersey 07621-0120.* VISA and MasterCard holders call 1-800-253-6476 to order Penguin titles.

IN CANADA: Please write to *Penguin Books Canada Ltd, 10 Alcorn Avenue, Suite 300, Toronto, Ontario M4V 3B2.*

IN AUSTRALIA: Please write to *Penguin Books Australia Ltd, P.O. Box 257, Ringwood, Victoria 3134.*

IN NEW ZEALAND: Please write to *Penguin Books (NZ) Ltd, Private Bag 102902, North Shore Mail Centre, Auckland 10.*

IN INDIA: Please write to *Penguin Books India Pvt Ltd, 706 Eros Apartments, 56 Nehru Place, New Delhi 110 019.*

IN THE NETHERLANDS: Please write to *Penguin Books Netherlands bv, Postbus 3507, NL-1001 AH Amsterdam.*

IN GERMANY: Please write to *Penguin Books Deutschland GmbH, Metzlerstrasse 26, 60594 Frankfurt am Main.*

IN SPAIN: Please write to *Penguin Books S. A., Bravo Murillo 19, 1° B, 28015 Madrid.*

IN ITALY: Please write to *Penguin Italia s.r.l., Via Felice Casati 20, I-20124 Milano.*

IN FRANCE: Please write to *Penguin France S. A., 17 rue Lejeune, F-31000 Toulouse.*

IN JAPAN: Please write to *Penguin Books Japan, Ishikiribashi Building, 2-5-4, Suido, Bunkyo-ku, Tokyo 112.*

IN GREECE: Please write to *Penguin Hellas Ltd, Dimocritou 3, GR-106 71 Athens.*

IN SOUTH AFRICA: Please write to *Longman Penguin Southern Africa (Pty) Ltd, Private Bag X08, Bertsham 2013.*